WAVENOMICS

RIDING THE STOCK MARKET WAVES THE WAY YOUR FINANCIAL ADVISOR IS PAID NOT TO TELL YOU

INVESTWAVES LLC

FOREWORD

This book has been over a year in the making. There is so much to say about investing today, so many ideas and thoughts to get across its hard to know where to start. What's the most important point to get across? It was paralysis brought on by information overload. Do we tell you everything we learned from an advisor who spent over 30 years in the financial services business? And make no mistake – it IS a business! Designed to first and foremost generate fees and commissions.

They said they're not against fees and commissions, and neither are we. Where we part company with the industry standard is when the drive for revenue runs over the people they are supposed to help.

So, the best way to start anything is to start! We're going to let the thoughts come and try to capture them before they pass by and the next thought takes its place. We're not going to try and give you all that we've learned from our 'inside source', but enough to hopefully make a difference. If we like the results, maybe we'll do another book. But if we continue to wait for the perfect book, there will be no book at all.

What follows are stories, anecdotes, and insights shared by our industry veteran. Some of it isn't pretty. In fact, some of the experiences they shared about their time with a major insurance company are downright ugly. So here we go. First person stories shared with us by a 30 plus year veteran, not afraid to share some inside secrets.

When the first person ("I") is used, those are direct anecdotes from this industry veteran. They'll pop up a lot throughout the book.

We dedicate this book to the Wave Riders. Individuals who are working hard, and want their money to work hard for them, and could use some help to protecting themselves from the talking heads on the financial news channels spewing propaganda designed mostly to keep under informed investors in the markets at all times and at all costs.

We hope you benefit from our discoveries, and the facts, anecdotes, and information we were able to gather from our secret weapon – someone who has been successful inside the financial industry for over thirty years and wanted to share the truth with us. Who wanted to make sure that everyone had access to the tools and information to become a better investor.

CHAPTER 1

IT'S ABOUT TRUST

THE FINANCIAL SERVICES industry is based on trust. You only have to look back to 2008 to see what happens when trust evaporates.

During the housing crisis, nobody knew how to value the toxic mix of loans and derivatives that the investment banks had manufactured. When people didn't trust the valuations the entire financial market nearly came to a screeching halt. There were many other reasons for the collapse, but there are also many books written on the subject so no need to repeat them here.

But this is why you often hear the exact same thing repeated over and over again from the Heads (*that's 'Talking Heads'*) on the financial programs. Their jobs, and the industry as it currently functions, depends on you to have confidence in the system. However, from some points of view that confidence is waning. From our point of view this is not necessarily a bad thing. We believe that any solid growth, whether in the economy as a whole, or your portfolio in particular, must be built upon a foundation of truth. Otherwise it is destined for collapse.

In 2000 – 2002 we saw a collapse based on a rotten foundation of hyped up earnings projections. In 2008 the rotten foundation was housing valuations and the mistaken belief that house prices only went up.

In order to keep the charade going, you need actors whose own image and public perception are tied to it. One of the best examples we can think of is a very old story from our childhood, *The Emperor's New Clothes*. We'd like to share it with you here. Take the time to read it, even if you've read it before – the moral of the story is the heart of this book.

THE EMPEROR'S NEW CLOTHES, BY HANS CHRISTIAN ANDERSEN

Many years ago, there was an Emperor so exceedingly fond of new clothes that he spent all his money on being well dressed. He cared nothing about reviewing his soldiers, going to the theatre, or going for a ride in his carriage, except to show off his new clothes. He had a coat for every hour of the day, and instead of saying, as one might, about any other ruler, "The King's in council," here they always said. "The Emperor's in his dressing room."

In the great city where he lived, life was always gay. Every day many strangers came to town, and among them one day came two swindlers. They let it be known they were weavers, and they said they could weave the most magnificent fabrics imaginable. Not only were their colors and patterns uncommonly fine, but clothes made of this cloth had a wonderful way of becoming invisible to anyone who was unfit for his office, or who was unusually stupid.

"Those would be just the clothes for me," thought the Emperor. "If I wore them, I would be able to discover which men in my empire are unfit for their posts. And I could tell the wise men from the fools. Yes, I certainly must get some of the stuff woven for me right away."

He paid the two swindlers a large sum of money to start work at once.

They set up two looms and pretended to weave, though there was nothing on the looms. All the finest silk and the purest old thread which they demanded went into their traveling bags, while they worked the empty looms far into the night.

"I'd like to know how those weavers are getting on with the cloth," the Emperor thought, but he felt slightly uncomfortable when he remembered that those who were unfit for their position would not be able to see the fabric. It couldn't have been that he doubted himself, yet he thought he'd rather send someone else to see how things were going. The whole town knew about the cloth's peculiar power, and all were impatient to find out how stupid their neighbors were.

"I'll send my honest old minister to the weavers," the Emperor decided. "He'll be the best one to tell me how the material looks, for he's a sensible man and no one does his duty better."

So, the honest old minister went to the room where the two swindlers sat working away at their empty looms.

"Heaven help me," he thought as his eyes flew wide open, "I can't see anything at all". But he did not say so.

Both the swindlers begged him to be so kind as to come near to approve the excellent pattern, the beautiful colors. They pointed to the empty looms, and the poor old minister stared as hard as he dared.

He couldn't see anything, because there was nothing to see. "Heaven have mercy," he thought. "Can it be that I'm a fool? I'd have never guessed it, and not a soul must know. Am I unfit to be the minister? It would never do to let on that I can't see the cloth."

"Don't hesitate to tell us what you think of it," said one of the weavers.

"Oh, it's beautiful -it's enchanting." The old minister peered through his spectacles. "Such a pattern, what colors!" I'll be sure to tell the Emperor how delighted I am with it."

"We're pleased to hear that," the swindlers said. They proceeded to name all the colors and to explain the intricate pattern. The old minister paid the closest attention, so that he could tell it all to the Emperor. And so, he did.

The swindlers at once asked for more money, more silk and gold thread, to get on with the weaving. But it all went into their pockets. Not a thread went into the looms, though they worked at their weaving as hard as ever.

The Emperor presently sent another trustworthy official to see how the work progressed and how soon it would be ready. The same thing happened to him that had happened to the minister. He looked and he looked, but as there was nothing to see in the looms. He couldn't see anything.

"Isn't it a beautiful piece of goods?" the swindlers asked him, as they displayed and described their imaginary pattern.

"I know I'm not stupid," the man thought, "so it must be that I'm unworthy of my good office. That's strange. I mustn't let anyone find it out, though." So, he praised the material he did not see. He declared he was delighted with the beautiful colors and the exquisite pattern. To the Emperor he said, "It held me spellbound."

All the town was talking of this splendid cloth, and the Emperor wanted to see it for himself while it was still in the looms. Attended by a band of chosen men, among whom were his two old trusted officials-the ones who had been to the weavers-he set out to see the two swindlers. He found them weaving with might and main, but without a thread in their looms.

"Magnificent," said the two officials already duped. "Just look, Your Majesty, what colors! What a design!" They pointed to the empty looms, each supposing that the others could see the stuff.

"What's this?" thought the Emperor. "I can't see anything. This is terrible!

Am I a fool? Am I unfit to be the Emperor? What a thing to happen to me of all people!"

"Oh! It's very pretty," he said aloud. "It has my highest approval." And he nodded approbation at the empty loom. Nothing could make him say that he couldn't see anything.

His whole retinue stared and stared. One saw no more than another, but they all joined the Emperor in exclaiming, "Oh! It's very pretty," and they advised him to wear clothes made of this wonderful cloth especially for the great procession he was soon to lead. "Magnificent! Excellent! Unsurpassed!" were bandied from mouth to mouth, and everyone did his best to seem well pleased. The Emperor gave each of the swindlers a cross to wear in his buttonhole, and the title of "Sir Weaver."

Before the procession the swindlers sat up all night and burned more than six candles, to show how busy they were finishing the Emperor's new clothes. They pretended to take the cloth off the loom. They made cuts in the air with huge scissors. And at last they said, "Now the Emperor's new clothes are ready for him."

Then the Emperor himself came with his noblest noblemen, and the swindlers each raised an arm as if they were holding something. They said,

"These are the trousers, here's the coat, and this is the mantle," naming each garment. "All of them are as light as a spider web. One would almost think he had nothing on, but that's what makes them so fine."

"Exactly," all the noblemen agreed, though they could see nothing, for there was nothing to see.

"If Your Imperial Majesty will condescend to take your clothes off," said the swindlers, "we will help you on with your new ones here in front of the long mirror."

The Emperor undressed, and the swindlers pretended to put his new clothes on him, one garment after another. They took him around the waist and seemed to be fastening something - that was his train - as the Emperor turned round and round before the looking glass.

"How well Your Majesty's new clothes look. Aren't they becoming!" He heard on all sides, "That pattern, so perfect! Those colors, so suitable! It is a magnificent outfit."

Then the minister of public processions announced: "Your Majesty's canopy is waiting outside."

"Well, I'm supposed to be ready," the Emperor said, and turned again for one last look in the mirror.

"It is a remarkable fit, isn't it?" He seemed to regard his costume with the greatest interest.

The noblemen who were to carry his train stooped low and reached for the floor as if they were picking up his mantle. Then they pretended to lift and hold it high. They didn't dare admit they had nothing to hold.

So off went the Emperor in procession under his splendid canopy.

Everyone in the streets and the windows said, "Oh, how fine are the Emperor's new clothes! Don't they fit him to perfection? And see his long train!" Nobody would confess that he couldn't see anything, for that would prove him either unfit for his position, or a fool. No costume the Emperor had worn before was ever such a complete success.

"But he hasn't got anything on," a little child said.

"Did you ever hear such innocent prattle?" said its father. And one person whispered to another what the child had said, "He hasn't anything on. A child says he hasn't anything on."

"But he hasn't got anything on!" the whole town cried out at last.

The Emperor shivered, for he suspected they were right. But he thought, "This procession has got to go on." So he walked more proudly than ever, as his noblemen held high the train that wasn't there at all.

YOU DEAR READER MAY BE THE EMPEROR!

Your 'clothes' are all of the notions and beliefs you've been told over the years about investing. When the Heads come along and tell you they have the answers to your portfolio needs, but only the wise and prudent can possibly understand how it all works, it is nearly impossible to admit that you don't get it at all, for then you would be admitting to them that you are neither wise or prudent.

When they tell you that you have to live with serious losses from time to time and there's no way to avoid them if you're going to wear the clothes (be invested in the markets), what choice do you have but to believe them?

So, you turn to your trusted advisors, who have been fed the same line. And while they may inwardly know that it is bunk, how can they be the first to say it isn't so.

For then they might lose their position. This story is more like the financial industry than most will admit. Our advisor friend has a reputation in certain circles for speaking when those in charge would rather they didn't – like the time they were told NOT to correct a mis-deed done by a previous agent in hopes that the 80-something year old lady would die before they had to do something (this incident eventually led to his resignation out of disgust), or when he stood up in an auditorium full of insurance agents and pointed out to the audience that what the speaker was telling them to do was illegal – and nearly got fired.

It may be that your advisor is telling you what the industry demands that they say. They repeat what is handed down to them to help them **play their primary role – to keep you fully invested at all times**.

He told us how when, during the 2002 and the 2008 crisis', he received memo's from his back office telling him what to say to clients during these difficult times. Now, coming from major national firms you would expect sage advice on how to protect client assets, to mitigate losses, or some other savvy investment advice.

No.

The memos contained platitudes and talking points designed to keep clients fully invested during the crisis. 'Remind your clients that investing is a long term proposition and losses and corrections are a normal part of the experience', 'Remember that if you miss the 10 best days during the last 20 years your average annual returns fall from 'X%' to a heck of a lot less than 'X%'".

He wanted to puke, and could barely take it.

That was 2002. Someone once said that oftentimes it takes a bad experience to put us in position to have a good experience. Whoever said that certainly said it way more elegantly, but you get the point. For us, it sparked the development of the system now used by InvestWaves.

This book contains the thoughts and ideas that together comprise the InvestWaves methodology. A financial discipline that strives to be invested during rising markets and seeks to avoid falling markets; promoting the idea that the best way to improve investment returns may be to avoid large losses over time.

We want to leave you with one last story to keep in mind before diving into the rest of the book. In the early 1900s, there was a man who worked at a place called a "bucket shop." Under fire in the early 20th century and illegal today, bucket shops were places where a poor man with little money could "invest" in the stock market by betting on daily price fluctuations. However, when these men sold or purchased stock at a bucket shop, that money was never invested in the stock market, but rather, remained "in the bucket" of the shop, to be played back and forth between the bucket shop and its various clients. More often than not, bucket shops were scams—think of the penny-stock "investment shop" the Wolf of Wall Street worked at when he first began.

Anyway, this man in the early 1900s had a unique way of looking at the price movements and could "win" against the shops more often than not. He became so good at their game that one by one, the bucket shops banned him from investing with them. He became wealthy and went to Wall Street where, after some time, he adapted his style and was successful there as well.

What, exactly, did he do? He timed his purchases, learning when to get in, and when to get out. He cared very little for earnings reports, profit and loss statements, and all the invisible fabric that goes into investing decisions today. Looking at them, he was the little boy that said, "there's nothing there." We are trying to tell people today the same thing.

CHAPTER 2

A DINNER PARTY

I HAD SETTLED into my seat around the cloth-covered round table, polishing off a frisée salad before the waiters brought out intricately arranged plates of filet mignon with mushroom ragout and shallot-roasted asparagus, and a steaming mound of garlic mashed potatoes. Of course, a nice glass of wine was offered, and like clockwork, the sommeliers generously poured and refilled glasses as soon as they noticed a deficit.

We always eat well at these events. What events, you may ask? Just the usual dinner sponsored by an investment product vendor, where investment professionals are "wined and dined," then treated to a long and detailed presentation of the sponsor's investment product. If it sounds nefarious, believe me—it isn't. I don't know of anyone who really sells a product to their client because someone bought them dinner. And no matter how good the meal is, sitting through one of these events is painful enough to cancel out any lingering effects of goodwill generated by wine and food.

Anyway, this particular dinner party was in October of 2010. I'm seated at a table full of advisors, and naturally the discussion turned to the recent market meltdown that launched the recession in 2008.

"How did you make out?" was the question going around the table, and we all listened as each told their story of grief and sorrow, followed by a cheerful but very revealing statement: "Although the markets were down almost 50%, my clients were *only* down about 40%, so we did really well, saving them 10% of losses."

This was actually said with a smile and was greeted with approving nods all around. Wow! Congratulations! You saved your clients 10% of losses! And as each in turn gave basically the same tale of grief and pain followed by a similar upbeat assessment of their performance, I became more and more anxious to share my experience.

"How about you? How did you do?" I was ready!

I had my answer and was eager to fill them in on the hows and whys – all of the details that would change the way they think about investment strategies. "Well," I began, "We went to cash in the fall of 2007, so we only lost about 6% or so. For the most part, we sat on the sidelines watching the carnage, until the Spring of 2009."

You should have seen the look on their faces! Was it shock? Awe? Or admiration? Definitely admiration. No, wait...that's not it...was it...wait, what *was* it? How do you describe a blank stare? Disinterest? Apathy? Really, you could have heard a cricket chirp in the deafening silence that ensued. I swallowed a forkful of mashed potatoes and I swear the sound of it going down my throat could be heard around the room.

I, of course, was sitting there with a look of hopeful expectation. We had just gone through the *second* massive market meltdown (hereafter referred to as MMM) in our lifetime (anyone remember the 2000-2002 bursting of the Internet bubble?) and I had successfully navigated it. *Certainly,* they would be begging me to find out what prompted me to get out when I did. They *must* want to know how, exactly, I did it, and whether or not I could share my knowledge? Nope. Not one question. The guy sitting to my left took a sip of his wine, the person who had originally posed the question looked away and kind of fumbled with his napkin, and the next person to speak asked the guy to my right, "So how did YOU do?" He of course repeated almost exactly what the others had said.

Think about your own profession for a moment. If you were at an event attended by your peers, and you had just gone through a very difficult period that adversely affected your industry, and you heard someone say that they figured out a way *not* to experience the pain that you just went through, wouldn't you want to know how they did it?

It took me a long time to get over that experience. I'm the type of person who needs to know why people respond the way they do – to figure out what makes them tick, to understand the motives behind their actions (or in this case, reaction). This experience was repeated many times over the years, under differing circumstances. Each time I expected to be asked, '" How did you do that, and can I do it too?"

The closest I came to such a response was when I invited an advisor to have coffee with me, and to discuss the possibility of working together. He worked in the small business retirement market, setting up 401(k) plans, etc. We met at a local coffee shop one morning in January of 2012. I showed him my chart (see the appendix) – depicting the strategy I had successfully developed before the market crash of 2008, the one that helped me to avoid the tremendous losses of that crash, the one that I thought would change the way advisors do business. I explained in broad strokes how I do my research and some of the methods I use.

For the first time I had an audience that actually seemed interested. He seemed to be taking it all in, studying the chart, commenting on the areas that showed where I moved client assets to the relative safety of money market funds and cash. I was ecstatic. YES! I had finally found a sympathetic ear!

He finished with the chart and looked up at me. As he began to speak, I think I must have inched forward in my chair. I couldn't wait to hear his solid agreement that I had uncovered something unique and valuable. Something that would help our clients reach their financial goals. "Geeze, this is great, but it looks pretty hard. I don't think it's something I would want to try and explain to my clients."

InvestWaves here again. Our friend told us it all went fuzzy after that. They've tried since then to get others in the investment industry to understand what he was doing, but the response was generally the same. As you read through this little book, we'll introduce you to some of the people he introduced us to. There's "Spiff Peterman," the perfect advisor. He's the quintessential, likable good guy—when he met him, he found *himself* wanting to throw money at him to invest. Then there's "Harry Wholesaler", who called him one day wanting him to consider letting *his* firm manage his clients' money. Harry was actually very helpful and put our friend on the path of healing. You'll meet him too.

But in the end, here is what we determined to be true: Advisors are like wildebeests. They go where the herd goes, and the herd goes where the herd has always gone. We want to help you break free from the herd mentality.

Imagine a herd of wildebeests watching one of their own *not* wander into the tall grass to be eaten by the lion.... "Hey you! Yes, you, the guy avoiding this tall grass here. Where do you think *you're* going? What? You want to avoid the grass because in the past you've seen wildebeests get eaten by the lions who are hiding in there? What's wrong with you?! Being eaten is part of being a wildebeest! How dare you refuse to subject yourself to the possibility! It's un-wildebeest, we'll ostracize you, and you'll be a pariah! Get back here and throw your lot in here with the rest of us!"

Are you a wildebeest? When your advisor tells you that severe losses are all a part of investing and they can't be avoided, do you follow along because, well, that's just what investors do? After seeing portfolios decimated time and time again, have you just come to accept that this is the way it is? Or are you willing to try and avoid the tall grass?

If someone walked up to you and said there was a way to at least _try_ to not lose so much of your hard-fought gains in the market, would you listen, or would you follow blindly after the herd?

The thing about the herd is that you can't tell one wildebeest from the other. If one gets himself eaten it wasn't really his fault. So, in that way there is safety in the herd. Safety from being singled out as "wrong", As long as everyone else is wrong too and you're willing to be eaten alive.

Stick with us here. We're going to show you how you could actually go your own way and survive, maybe even thrive.

CHAPTER 3

'SPIFF PETERMAN'

I HAD ACCEPTED an invitation to participate in a Continuing Education course sponsored by an investment company I had done some business with. The course was entitled, 'Retirement Myths'. Sounded like something I would enjoy, plus I would get credit towards my course requirements which some states require to maintain professional licenses, as well as college requirements to maintain my professional designations.

Prior to the session I received in the mail a package containing a synopsis of the course along with the location, a CD containing a 700 page book, and instructions to 'read the book before attending the class.' You can imagine how far my jaw dropped when I popped the CD into the computer and saw that there were 700 pages to read!

I started in, and soon became engrossed in the material. The book was written by a MIT engineer turned financial advisor. And he knew his stuff! He methodically debunked nearly every single method of investing sold to the public by Oreo advisors (more on Oreos later).

I found I couldn't stop reading. I was fascinated by his methodology and his conclusions. Why?

Because these were the SAME conclusions I had come to on my own! With solid math, graphs, and high-level MIT engineering analysis to back it up! What I had come to understand on my own was now being laid out in highly detailed, methodical and logical arguments. I had found my textbook. I printed it out – all 700 pages - and keep it to this day on my conference table and refer to it from time to time. I was ready for the class, and the exam.

The class and subsequent test were being held at a Golf Club. I had never been there before but had an idea of where it was located, having driven through the area many times when I'd visit my son who was attending university in the city at the time.

I pulled off the exit and drove through the bucolic neighborhood, admiring some of the homes and the marvelous landscaping on the way to the club. You could tell that there was a lot of money in these homes – definitely an 'upper crust' vibe. A 'Benz parked in the driveway was not a status symbol here, it was expected.

I found the club with no problem and parked a few rows back from the door. I was very early. I usually am at these things. I like to be able to choose my seat – always facing the speaker if the tables are round, outside table with easy access to the restroom. If you're a guy anywhere near 50 years old, you understand.

The facilities were beautiful. Just what you'd expect situated in the neighborhood it was a part of. I walked in through the front door and to my right a long table was set up with a white linen cover and a sign that said 'Registration'. There was a sign in sheet, materials for the meeting and right in front manning the table was a familiar face! It's always a pleasant surprise to see someone you know and haven't seen for a while. I had met him in New York about a year prior. It was his company that was sponsoring the event, but I had no idea he would be there that day.

We chatted a bit, getting caught up on what was new with each other. I registered, gathered my materials and headed off to secure my prime location when I paused, turned around and said to my friend, 'By the way, thanks for the book. I really enjoyed it!' He looked at me with the oddest expression on his face and replied, 'You read the book? No one reads the book. Dude, it's 700 pages!' I laughed and went to my seat, thinking what a jokester he was.

Soon the room began to fill up. Most of the people were from the local area, and several of them knew a lot of the attendees. I think they probably go to a lot of these meetings together. The presenter went to the front of the room and gave us the meeting guidelines. Because this was an official state sanctioned event offering CE credits, there were rules – strict ones. Yes sir! The course began. It was a one-hour lecture, to be followed by the exam.

When the lecture was over my friend passed out the testing materials: a booklet (sealed – don't open it until I say 'begin') and the obligatory #2 pencils – two of them of course. We were told that one hour was allotted for the test, but the average time was 45 minutes. If you hit the 45-minute mark and are less than half way through you may want to hurry, because blank answers are automatically marked wrong. Better to hurry up and finish than leave it blank.

Got it?

OK, begin!

To be fair, I'm a pretty good test taker. Always have been. I'm the kid you grew up with that always finished the test first, got an 'A', and screwed up the 'curve'. I knew it, and if I'm being honest, I was kind of proud of it. In middle school there was this girl, Janet, who would sometimes beat me to the finish. I didn't like Janet~

So, I wasn't surprised when, 20 minutes after 'Begin!', I was done. I didn't know what to do. No one told us the proper procedure for turning in the exam, and since it was an official state approved exam, I was sure there was one. There always is. I raised my hand.

My friend noticed my lone hand before complete numbness set in.

My friend: 'Ah, yes...?'

Me: 'I'm done. What should I do with the exam?'

My friend – same odd expression he had when I told him I had read the book: You're..... done?'

Me: 'Yes, I read the book, remember?'

He came and collected my exam and testing materials, and I quietly exited the room, aware of the familiar glares piercing the back of my scull from the eyes of those struggling to finish in time. Since I hadn't used the restroom yet, and remember I am 50ish, prudence dictated that I do so before leaving for my two-hour drive home. Unfortunately for me, the facilities were clear on the other side of the building.

By the time I found it, took care of business, and got back to the front doors, other people had started finishing up. As I was nearing the door a tall, well-dressed gentleman was coming out of the testing area and we were going to reach the door together. This guy was awesome! He had on a $3,000 suit, monogramed shirt, diamond cufflinks and not a single hair out of place. This guy LOOKED like the textbook successful financial advisor. He was SPIFFY. Let me introduce you to Spiff Peterman.....

'What did you think?', I asked him.

'It was depressing', he offered.

'Why?', I asked.

He said, 'According to the MIT guy, and the testing material, we have absolutely NOTHING of value to offer to our clients. Nothing that we tell them really works in the real world!' He really did look depressed.

I asked him. 'Didn't you read chapter 17? That's where he talks about the one thing that really CAN improve our clients' investment performance – TIMING!'

'No', he said, 'I didn't read the book. I mean, I started to, but there was too much math in it for me. I couldn't finish it.'

OK, just let that sink in for a moment.... Here is this obviously successful guy. He looked so good *I* wanted to give him some money to invest!

And he didn't read a book on investing because it had too much math in it?

Imagine walking into your doctor's office and being thoroughly impressed with all of the very large, leather bound books lining the dark walnut shelves of his collegiate collection. I love the smell of books, and *those* types of books convey a weighty impression of knowledge. You make mention to the doctor how impressed you are, and she replies, 'Oh yes, they look very nice. Of course, I've never read any of them. There's too much biology and stuff like that in them. Now, let's talk about your upcoming surgery....'

That's how I felt, at the moment, about Spiff.

It was frightening to imagine how many people were trusting this guy with their life savings, their children's inheritance, and their financial wellbeing, and he wouldn't read a manual on investing strategies and techniques because there was too much math.

Did you know, that to become an 'investment professional' requires just a few weeks of study and a 70% passing grade on a couple of relatively easy tests?

That's right, you can **_NOT KNOW_** 30% of the material, and be able to take control of a person's investments.

I don't know about you, but I think that's scary stuff.

By the way, Spiff passed the exam.....

CHAPTER 4

OREO'S AND CHOCOLATE CHIP COOKIES

I WAS FEELING A LITTLE FRUSTRATED. My wife and I were at an event and someone I had just met asked me what I did for a living. 'I manage investments', I offered. 'Ohhhh', she nodded knowingly. Then she began lecturing me on how she lost money in the markets, it's all gambling, and most of 'you' (myself excluded of course) are getting rich off of the little guy while they – the little guy – makes little or no money. I was frustrated because this lady was, in my opinion, mostly right. And because I don't do business like 'most of them', and she was lumping me in along with the rest.

'Wait', you may be saying. 'Did you just write that the lady was right?'

Yes.

I did.

She is.

Well, to an extent anyway. A lot of people treat investing like gambling. It's the wrong approach and will, more often than not, lose your money for you. Study after study has shown that the average investor doesn't do well with investing, and on an inflation adjusted basis barely breaks even. Yet their advisor drives a nice car, lives in a nice house in the best neighborhood. I couldn't disagree with her about 'you people', except I'm not one of 'them'! But how do I say that? I was at the same time embarrassed for my industry and proud of all the ways I was different, but how do I make people see?

And my dear, patient, saintly wife (trying to score some points here!) was letting me vent. She had actually heard me talk about this perception problem that I have many times before. Then she said something that helped me more than she realized. 'You're like finding a chocolate chip cookie in a box of Oreos!' That was it! I don't know if it makes sense to you, but it was clear as day to me. I just let that sink in for a few moments. She knows me so well. I'm a visual person who better understands things in pictures, and she just painted the Sistine Chapel for me!

Imagine you are in a store, and you're looking for cookies for your kids' lunches. Everyone knows what Oreos are. Heck, you better! Nabisco spends a bazillion dollars a year advertising them. It'd be a shame to think they were wasting all that money. You open the box labeled 'Oreos', and there are no surprises: Black cookies with white cream filling – blackwhiteblackwhiteblackwhite – they're all the same.

Well, the financial industry spends a bazillion dollars a year telling you just what a 'financial advisor' is too. And they spend a lot of money on us making sure we understand as well.

If you've spoken with more than one financial advisor over the years, have you ever wondered why all of their advice sounds the same? When was the last time you really heard something original?

That's why I couldn't be upset with the woman who sort of went off on me. She was right, most advisors ARE alike. They give you basically the same talking points, because we all get them. When the markets are falling, we get memos telling us to make sure we let you, our clients, know to stay fully invested. If they suggest 'playing it safe', they may take the radical approach of moving maybe 5% or so of your portfolio to cash.

Didn't you ever wonder why, for example, when

the Heads say their analysis shows a strong probability of a 20% decline, they don't follow their own advice and just get out of the markets? I did. And I decided I wouldn't be an Oreo OR a wildebeest. It was this mindset that gave me the courage NOT to enter the tall grass in 2008, to at least TRY not to get eaten alive, while the rest of the herd was telling me I was crazy, to get back in with the rest of them and stop being 'different'.

So now I tell people that I'm like finding a chocolate chip cookie in a box of Oreos. You open the box labeled 'Advisor' and see they're basically all the same – blackwhiteblackwhiteblackwhite – WHOA! What's this?

This my friend, is InvestWaves. Come out of that tall grass, let's see if we can avoid being eaten.

DON'T TRUST THE TALKING HEADS

Let's play a game. Ten of us sit at desks scattered throughout a classroom. On the desk in front of us are four colored cups that are turned upside down. Out in the hallway are four players called 'Investment Opportunities' (IO's for short). They each have a bag of M&M's, with each bag containing only one color of M&M. The colored cups correspond to the colors of the M&M's – Green, Yellow, Red and Brown. The IO's take turns randomly entering the room one at a time, and only one can be in the room at any given time.

The object of the game is to gather as many M&M's as you can. You do this by trying to guess which IO is going to come into the room. When you think you know, and before they enter, you turn up the cup of the same color as the IO you believe will be entering. If you guess correctly, they'll drop a candy into your cup. If you have the wrong color turned up you are passed by and they may also TAKE a candy from you, meaning that you suffered a loss by your wrong choice.

So, each time you correctly pick the IO's move, your M&M stash grows. Pick wrong, and you may suffer a loss. Hopefully you can see where this is going. It bears some resemblance to investing, right? Now you might argue that investing involves more than chance and I would agree with you. But bear with me for purposes of my illustration.

Now suppose, out of the ten players in the room, two or three seem to be doing better than the others. They begin offering their opinion on which IO will be coming next, and the rest of the players begin following their tips. Keep in mind, the anointed 'experts' are still playing. Let me ask you: What incentive do the 'experts' have in giving the other players information that will ultimately diminish their own final tally of M&M's? Once the IO's run out of M&M's the game is over, the candies are counted and the one with the most wins. Suppose there is a pattern that the IO's are following. Maybe the experts noticed that if more than four players guess wrong, Green always comes in next. The experts would then have an incentive to try and make at least four players guess wrong, so they could pick up a green M&M on the next round!

Now let's look at a real life example: The 'Talking Heads' of the financial media. You know who I mean if you've ever channel surfed, or are a diehard do it yourself investor. Like the crazy guy with the sound effects who screams BUYBUYBUY if he likes a stock, or SELLSELLSELL if he doesn't. There are so many of them, and if you watch long enough you are bound to get conflicting information.

There was one show – I don't know if it's still on air – where they had a panel of experts. Each one would give their opinion on where a stock's price would move and when it would do it. They rarely agreed. What's the point?!

Early in my career I used to watch these guys as I was getting ready for work. High powered CEO's coming on camera to give us the inside scoop on their company so we could rush to our computers to enter buy orders as soon as the market opens. WOW! This is information I can use to help my clients' portfolios do better! Only, it wasn't. And it didn't. I stopped watching. You should stop watching too.

There is a book I would like to recommend.

Reminiscences of a Stock Operator by Edwin Lefevre. It is a biography about legendary stock investor Jesse Livermore. How he got started in the investment business, and lessons he learned along the way. In it the author gives several accounts of the 'Talking Heads' of his day and his dealings with them. Basically, his conclusion is that they are manipulating you in some way at the worst, and at best the information they give is useless.

Look, if the price of a stock can be affected by new information, and I will tell you it can, what good is information that is already available to thousands of other people and every professional trader in the markets?? If the big Talking Head is telling you about it, the news has already been priced into the stock. And as a side note: If they are giving you information that can materially impact the price of a stock, and that information is not available to the general public, it is illegal to trade on that information! It's called insider trading. Ask Martha Stewart. She went to prison for it.

What I have found over the years is too much information causes your decision-making function to short circuit. It can paralyze you or cause you to second guess your analysis. Be very careful where you get your information from and limit the amount of information to just what you need to make an informed decision. Trust me, I learned this the hard way.

CHAPTER 5

THERAPY

CERTAIN THINGS just drive me nuts. My family can confirm that one of my favorite phrases ("I feel like I'm taking crazy pills!") from the movie *Zoolander* is uttered *ad nauseam*, in instances both fitting and not, around the house. But sometimes the situation demands it, and I can't find a more encompassing expression. Doing what I do in this industry, you can't help but feel that everyone around you is insane, that Blue Steel and Magnum are *totally* the same face, that if people *really knew* the process behind investing and money management, they wouldn't be making some of the decisions they do.

For instance...

The other day I was attending a routine business meeting. I take part in several local networking groups, which meet weekly to promote businesses, share contacts, conduct charitable works, spread community awareness--and just generally provide each other with the support network that is crucial to engendering success and good will in a community.

Although our early morning weekday breakfasts convene rather earlier than I myself would prefer, I thoroughly enjoy being a part of these groups, have been helped and helped others many times, have significantly grown my business, and have made some of my closest friends as a result of these meetings. They're something I look forward to, even as I stumble out of bed and leave before I have time to make coffee.

So, I walked into our weekly Tuesday morning breakfast meeting, which is held in the conference room of a nearby hotel. It's a typical meeting, nothing special—probably all over America people are meeting in similar conference rooms around the same time, having similar conversations and eating similar food. The usual faux-wood tables are lined up around the edge of the room where the white-washed walls meet the gray carpet.

On one side lays a spread of typical "hot" breakfast items—scrambled egg soup, mysteriously-gray sausage patties and links, "crispy" bacon, a vat of oatmeal that might have been made yesterday, and what I *think* was an attempt at French toast (sticks). On the other side you have what my daughter calls "cheat day eats" - large plastic-glass trays of cream cheese Danishes stuffed with your choice of cherries or apricots, sugar coated yeast doughnuts, blueberry muffins, and cornflakes or grape-nuts next to pitchers of milk.

To the back, another table is lined with the necessary morning beverages – black coffee with cream and sugar packets and those little red stir straws, assorted teas, orange juice, grapefruit juice, and this thing called "decaf" which I've heard of but have never tried.

In the center of the room are a couple of long tables pushed together length-wise and encircled by about 25-30 cushioned chairs with metal legs; the format is round-table discussion, with members taking rotating turns as moderator and keynote presenter each week.

It's still slightly early; some people have taken their seats at the long central table and are chatting or looking through notes in books, phones, and tablets; some people are standing in the empty spaces in the room, deep in conversation with colleagues, hands clasped around cozy Styrofoam cups containing the elixir of life (coffee); some people are still trickling in, while others are picking their poison (literally—which one is LESS likely to give me food poisoning, the scrambled egg soup or Oliver Twist Oatmeal?). I opt for a seemingly-harmless Costco pre-fab cherry Danish and a cup of coffee, and head over to say hello and catch up with one of my good friends, who is swiping through his tablet, presumably reading the news or researching whether or not E. Coli can survive in tepid temperatures on a plate of half-eaten scrambled eggs.

We started talking, about the usual stuff—wives, kids, last night's baseball game and the like—when a woman came up and tapped me on the shoulder. She broke into our conversation as I was mid-sip, talking with my friend, by literally TAPPING ME ON THE SHOULDER like a kid asking her kindergarten teacher if she can go to the bathroom.

I turned to look, squinting to figure out who was interrupting our intense discussion about a recent baseball trade. It was a short, rather stout older woman with short, curly gray hair that matched the gray in the carpet and the gray on the metal cushioned seats. It was her saccharine pink skirt suit, however, that demanded your attention.

"I'm Mary Jacobs, and I live up near the lodge on

Bay Ridge Road. I just wanted to tell you to take me off your mailing list."

Now I've seen Mary around at the meetings, but I couldn't point her out in a crowd. I really had no idea who she was, asking me to take her off my mailing list. I didn't even know she was *on* the mailing list.

At this point I'm still a little too surprised to get annoyed by the extremely early-morning, pre-coffee, mid-discussion interruption from a woman that I couldn't pick out of a lineup, to ask me to take her off of my mailing list, which at *most* sends out maybe six mailings a year. One every two months. Because I get it—people don't like to get junk mail. *I* don't like to get junk mail. That's why my mailings are relatively infrequent, and why I try to keep them interesting. In fact, I've never had anyone ask to be removed or express annoyance, in all the 25-plus years I've been in business sending out mailings.

So anyway, I responded to Mary, "Of course, thanks for letting me know. As soon as I get back to my office, I'll make sure to take care of it for you." And I turned back to finish the conversation I was having with my friend.

"Ahem, ahem," I heard behind me, someone

pointedly clearing their throat. I was beginning to think Dolores Umbridge was in the room.

"Yes, Spiff Peterman is our financial advisor, and we're very happy with him, he takes good care of us. We're related…" she trailed off.

"Um, okay…" I responded.

She opened her mouth to add something else but before she could say any more the group president called the meeting to order. We all took our seats and the meeting commenced as we choked back swigs of "coffee" and did our best to provide feedback as the speaker presented his latest product development. But I was a little distracted. I had this lady on my mind, and I certainly didn't want to forget her request. I had a feeling that if, heaven forbid, I had *failed* to remove her from my mailing list, I'd most likely be hearing from her. *Ahem, ahem.* So, the first thing I did when I got back to the office was to inform my assistant.

"Missy, can you please take a woman named Mary Jacobs off of our mailing list?"

"Who?"

Exactly.

"Mary Jacobs, she asked to be removed."

"Sure thing."

Now normally, when something like this

happens, you get over it and move on—you can't win 'em all, so you let it go and get back to work. But I got to thinking later...what do you mean "he takes good care of you?"

Is Spiff watching your accounts daily, monitoring everything to make sure he has your best financial interests at heart? Because I actually *know* Spiff Peterman; I've seen Spiff's work and I've taken clients from Spiff– and I know that that's not the case. Does he watch your account positions, daily? Does he do market analysis, daily? Does he alert you when that analysis indicates that markets may be in a downward trend, and that it may be a good time to move to a cash position?

Does he inform you when there is a downturn in the markets, and that you might want to move that money tucked away in your 401k to a safer place? Is that what you mean when you say that you're being taken care of?

And this is where I feel like I'm taking crazy pills —because I *know* he doesn't do that for you. So, then what's your definition of "taking care of" someone? Maybe what Mary relative-of-Spiff means is that he fills out paperwork for her when she calls. Or maybe he sends her a card on her birthday. Is that the level of care she's talking about? Or better yet, perhaps she means that he tells her it's okay when her account is down 20%, 30% or more—not to worry, ol' Spiff is there to watch the losses so you don't have to! Advising you to 'just hang in there' and everything will be fine.

I've actually received those types of emails from companies with whom I have client money invested, where following a market downturn they essentially say "now here's what to say to your clients so that they stay with you and don't jump ship now that the markets are down 30%." I'm sure Spiff gets those emails too, so maybe when she says, "he takes good care of me," she means that he reads the company script and breaks the news gently, holding her hand as he tells her she's just lost a boat load of money. Top-notch customer care and client service, that is.

Now I realize that Spiff Peterman is a relative, so the circumstances in Mary's case are a little bit different. But I did have a man in my office recently, another client of Spiff; and Spiff apparently told him that he would "watch his account" before proceeding to lose almost half his money for him when the markets tanked in 2000/2001. Naturally the guy was a bit shell shocked and stayed out of the markets for a long time.

As if to add insult to injury, the markets then

turned around and rebounded—and this man was out when they did, so he was unable to capitalize on the upswing. Not only did he lose a ton of money, but he also lost out on an opportunity to make any of it back as well.

So, when one of my clients referred him to me, and I told him that I would watch his account, he was understandably skeptical. As soon as I said those words, his body had an almost physical reaction to them so that, back arched, hair standing on end, claws out, he kind of looked like one of those cliché black cat lawn decorations you see on Halloween, nearly hissing out "that's what the last guy said to me" in response.

"When the markets tanked and I lost all this money," he began telling me the story, "I called Spiff, and I said 'what do you mean you've lost nearly half of my investment—I thought you were watching this account!'"

"Listen, I have a lot of clients and a lot of accounts," Spiff told him; I have so many accounts, you don't understand—I can't just watch all of them like that."

Which is not to say that Spiff didn't watch this man's account at all; he just watched it go down until there was very little left.

He shifted uncomfortably in his armchair across the desk from me, peering at me intensely. I felt like he was the Sorting Hat, eyes squinting and wheels turning as he tried to determine which house to put me in, which group of advisors I belonged with—did I honor my word, or was I just out to get his money? Slytherin or Gryffindor? He looked at me again and said, "what do you *mean* you're gonna watch my account?"

The Oreo Advisor Standard is, basically, to review your quarterly statements when they come in. It's quite possible your advisor becomes aware of how your account is doing around the same time as you – when the quarterly statements arrive. How do I know this? I worked for a major financial firm before going out on my own and have been in this industry for nearly 30 years. Most advisors I've met are Spiff Petermans, whose primary goal is to get you to like and trust him so you'll give him your money.

That money is then sent off to a third-party money manager who doesn't know you, where they manage your money pretty much the same as all of the other managers. It's cookie cutter management, because after all, it's not natural to be different.

The other part of Spiff's job is to keep you happy and fully invested. He's the 'front man', and just like the Spiff I met at the educational meeting I mentioned earlier, may not know as much as he seems to. He or she (Spiff may just as well be a woman) dresses well, makes nice with you, gives you the information they are told to give when things are bad, and tries to get more money from you when things are good.

I explained to my soon to be new client how we try to avoid the tall grass (times of elevated risk in the markets) and have often watched from a safe place while others are getting eaten. I showed him the systems and strategy we employ. I shared the MIT engineer's book, where he determined 'Timing' was the only way to truly add value to a portfolio, as well as an article written by a Wall Street Journal contributor who shared a simple form of InvestWaves with his readers and stated that yes, it does in fact work.

He visibly relaxed, we signed some papers, and he's been on a diet of chocolate chip cookie for many years now.

CHAPTER 6

CAN I HELP YOU?

I WANT to begin this chapter by talking about the ubiquitous phrase "Can I Help You?"

We hear it all the time, usually when we're walking into a store—assuming that you get waited on, that is. It seems like half the time you walk into a store anymore the sales associates practically avoid eye contact, or mysteriously disappear into the break room, and it's like "Is anybody here?"

What I find funny is that sometimes you walk into a store and depending on who happens to be working that day, your experience with that store can be drastically different. One day you could get an extremely chipper "Hi! How are you?! Can I help you?!" from some perky young cashier who's probably had one too many cups of coffee, while other days, at the same store, you get a deadpan "Can I help you" that doesn't even end in a question mark, but rather in a period served with a side of annoyance.

There's a wide range of "Can I help you's" out there, which got me thinking: that phrase, when worded a certain way, or stated with a certain intonation, can convey many different meanings. It's usually meant to inquire about what you want, with the assumption that the asker is going to get whatever that may be. So whatever store you walk into, "Can I help you?" basically means "What are you here for, and can I get it for you?"

I'm going to turn that around just a little bit and talk about "***Can*** I help you," with an emphasis on my ability as an advisor to meet your specific needs as a client and an investor. This is a question that I try to answer as soon as we have our initial client interview. This process entails discussing a prospective client's situation and circumstances, and discerning whether or not my investing methodology is able to help the client. Unfortunately, as much as I wish I could, I can't help everyone.

I want to make it clear that me being able to help or not help a client has nothing to do with how much money he or she may currently have. I help people all the time who don't have much, or who are just starting out, so limited resources does not disqualify you from help.

Conversely, it also doesn't mean that I can't help you if you have too *much* money either. I had a couple come in recently with a large amount of money that they wanted to invest, and they asked me how much money I managed in total. After I told them the amount, they were like "Oh OK, this guy is comfortable handling large sums of money," and they then felt more at ease allowing me to work with their investments. My ability to help you has nothing to do with how much money you have or don't have.

Usually, in **my** business, "Can I help you?" refers to your attitude and your expectations.

So, let's talk to who I *can* help first.

Let's say you worked for 40 years at a large construction firm, and you've done a great job on your own. You've saved for retirement, and now it's time to put down the tools and finally enjoy the hard-earned fruits of your labor. Because you've already done a great job, and you've done some investing, you don't have unrealistic expectations. You're familiar with investments, you know how they work, you know there are cycles of ups and downs, and you have a good grasp of the basic concepts of investing;

you're used to climbing the mountain and building that nest egg, and now it's time to come down.

I read an interesting article about climbing Mount Everest while preparing a proposal for some clients, and it made me think about the parallels between investing and mountain climbing. These particular clients had worked hard to climb the proverbial mountain—they did all of the things I mentioned above to save for retirement and plan for the future.

They had inherited a business, and not only did they inherit it, but they grew it until it became a very large and profitable business, much larger and more successful than what they had initially received. Now, people that claim to "know" these people will often sneer and say "well they *inherited* all that, they think they're so great and entrepreneurial, but they *inherited* that business, they didn't do it on their own." But if they actually knew these people, they wouldn't be saying those things, because the truth is, they inherited a *small* business—a business that was a fraction of the size it currently is—and through their skill and their hard work and tireless effort, they built it up and grew it into a very nice business.

It is true, however, that stories like this are a rarity. Oftentimes when people inherit a business, they send it right down the drain, because they don't have the work ethic or know-how to nurture a business. So, if somebody inherits a business and is doing well, good for them!

So, these clients came to me, and knew that they were getting close to retirement; they had made the steep ascent up the mountain and were now getting ready for the bliss that would be the downhill glide. Which brings me back to the statistic I read about Mount Everest.

These days it seems like everyone is climbing Mount Everest, it's the Holy Grail of adventure seekers and mountain climbers. It's almost becoming a problem, with so many people climbing it now that there is an excess of foot traffic, garbage and litter everywhere, and I guess it's becoming quite chaotic. But despite the chaos of the climb and the almost competitive thirst to get to the top, most of the deaths occur on the descent—that's right, you read it correctly: *almost all of the deaths on Mount Everest occur on the descent.* People that have crested the summit, make it to the top, and die on the way down.

That's because descending Mount Everest is a whole new ball game. It's a different kind of climbing that requires a different set of skills. What happens on Everest is that people expend all of their energy and resources on getting to the top, and once they make it, they don't have enough to get them down. This flawed—and often lethal—approach is similar to one that people take with investing.

In investing, you sort of get into a mindset of accumulating, and when you hit retirement, you need to shift, because it's a different kind of investing; you need to switch into a different mindset that a lot of people just aren't used to.

If you're used to socking your money away in a 401k, that's the investing side of money management. You know how investments and 401(k)s work, but now you need to downshift into the retirement side of money management. Retirement can be very difficult for some people, so it's very important that when you hit that age where you're nearing retirement and you're leaving your job, that you talk to somebody who can help you successfully make that shift and come down the mountain that you've successfully climbed. Investing for income can be vastly different than investing for growth.

Here's another example of the type of people that I can help: small families. Maybe you're not quite ready for retirement, but the kids are gone, and you suddenly have more discretionary income than you thought possible. As much as we love them, kids are a huge drain on our resources. After all of the time and resources you spent building a family with strong family values, suddenly it's all yours again once the kids have flown the nest. So, for the past 18 or more years you've been responsible, you got your kids off to good start, you're in good shape financially, and now you have this extra money and time on your hands. Maybe you don't have a lot of savings, but you've got a good, newly available cash flow. If this is you—I can help you.

The last example I'm going to give you of a person I can help is the person who is just starting out in life. Let's say you graduated college and land your first decent "adult" job that allows you to live independently. You understand that the only person who is responsible for taking care of the older person you'll someday be is the younger person you are today. You want to be responsible and are willing to work towards your goal. If this is you, I can help you get there.

While everyone has a different story and set of circumstances that these scenarios can't fully encompass, they can be taken as basic molds intended to give a general sense of the different kinds of multifaceted people and scenarios that I can help. Now, as I mentioned before, there are a couple types of people that unfortunately, as much as I might wish to, I simply can't help.

So how do we figure out if I can help you?

We sit down, talk, and I ask you some probing questions to get a better sense of where you are and where you want to be. Now, if I *can't* help you, that doesn't make you a bad person, it doesn't reflect poorly on you as a person, and it doesn't mean that your situation is bad, hopeless, or irredeemable. It comes down to the way that I do business; I need to know that you're a good fit with my philosophy of investing and managing money.

One type of person that I can't help is a *desperate* person. Now, I don't mean that if your situation requires work, that I can't help you. What I'm referring to is more of an emotional state or mindset, an attitude of desperation. Unfortunately, I learned this the hard way.

A former business owner who'd recently lost everything to bankruptcy had come into my office, telling me that he had a lot of catching up to do. He told me his whole story; and it was a sad story, and some of the events which happened were a result of his choices, and some of them were circumstances beyond his control. Oftentimes this is the situation, and people need to understand that it's *completely fine*. It's okay. Sometimes life throws you curveballs and you react, and it may not be the best reaction but it's all you know how to do at the time.

Sometimes I have people that come in, and it's like using a rock to open up a can of beans – they just don't want to give me any information, and often it's because they're embarrassed by their current situation. Little do they know, I could share some moments of my life over the past 50 years that I'm not very proud of, or instances where I've made stupid decisions. That's called life, and we all make stupid decisions.

Sometimes there are circumstances beyond our control where you can make the right decision, but circumstances kind of slap you down. So, don't ever hesitate to come and talk to somebody because you're embarrassed of your current situation.

The fact that you're willing to talk about it and start making steps towards bettering your life and your situation, speaks very highly of you.

So anyway, this guy comes to have a consultation with me, and tells me "I have a lot of catching up to do, and I want to invest aggressively." He had a job, and he was making money, and he said, "I'm going to sock away a bunch of money—and I'm willing to take a high risk to do so."

"Okay...." I hesitated.

Something felt slightly off, but instead of listening to my gut I decided to follow through with an analysis.

After I ran the analysis, I showed it to him, and I showed him the rate of return that he would need to earn, and where we would have to invest in order to give him the _opportunity_ to achieve such a high rate of return. It's important to keep in mind that with investing, there are absolutely *no* guarantees. Some people equate risk with success, incorrectly thinking "I'm going to take a higher risk so I can earn more." Sometimes, in some cases, taking on excess risk does not mean that you will make more money. In fact, it can mean the opposite—it means you can lose what you already have.

I made sure to discuss this in depth and in advance with my prospective client, and indicated that such aggressive, high-risk investing is not really what I do. But it was what he wanted me to do. So, after we talked about it, I set him up with an account.

Now, this man didn't just want an account that he could set up and then leave alone; he wanted to be able to watch his accounts online. That was my first indicator that something was slightly off—not that I discourage people from taking an active interest in their investments but wanting to monitor any and every move is one possible indicator of a potentially restless or uneasy investor.

Again, ignoring my better instincts, we set up his investments and had one final appointment just before we launched everything, where we walked through the details one last time and I showed him how to access his accounts so he could monitor them online.

After going through everything, I said "Now these are going to fluctuate—they're RISKY—so these are going to fluctuate a *lot*. Don't watch them every day, because you will drive yourself nuts. Literally crazy. Do yourself a favor and do NOT watch these every day."

"Alright," he responded, "so what do you think I should do instead?"

"You know," I began, "A *lot* of monitoring would be checking your account once a month; that would maybe give you an idea of the general direction, but even that's probably more than most people do. But if you want to really keep an eye on it, I would say maybe once a month."

Now, what I didn't tell him was that I have access to a report—at the end of every two weeks I get a list of clients who log in and check their accounts showing the exact date and time that they monitored their account.

And from this list I saw that he watched his account every day.

Two and three times a day. Sometimes more. It made *me* nervous watching him watch his account!

Since most of my clients just wait for their quarterly reports before checking their account—and some don't even want online access—the list may only have 10 or 12 total clients a day. But when I'd get the report and skim down, I'd see this guy, and his name was on my list every single day, multiple times a day.

He'd check it in the morning before work, check it at lunch, check it when he came home from work and sometimes even before bed. He eventually wore himself out, and he bailed early on his plan, and that was the best thing for both of us.

So, if you need to get rich quick, buy yourself a lottery ticket, because that's not what the market is about, and that's certainly not what investing is about. If you're desperate, I can't help you.

If you're unrealistic, I can't help you.

I've got another story here for you, but fortunately I caught this one before it started.

There was a couple that came into my office who

wanted to retire early. Before they came to me, they had saved up what they believed to be enough money; they sold everything they owned and were going to buy two motorcycles and a motor home, and travel the country until they dropped.

Now, because they hadn't really saved enough money for this, they needed to earn about 12% on their investments to make this work. Because they didn't want to risk the chance of having to go back to work, they wanted 100% safety—in other words, no risk whatsoever. And because they were "on the road" and sometimes emergencies pop up, they needed 100% liquidity—they didn't want any of the money locked up in investments that couldn't be turned quickly into cash. Basically, what they were asking for was an FDIC insured checking account paying 12% interest! A little bit unrealistic, to say the least!

I couldn't help them, so I let them know that this wasn't something that I could do.

Now, just because you have these issues doesn't mean that I'm not going to try to help you overcome them or just kick you to the door. Sometimes desperation comes from having goals that are too lofty, so part of our process is helping you see what is actually doable. The same thing goes for unrealistic expectations, which can be very harmful to your financial health. Unrealistic expectations can cause you not to save enough because you think you're going to earn more than is probable; in a vicious cycle that feeds off of itself, such behavior can then cause you to take on even *more* risk because you know you're not saving enough, so you get extra risky—all the while closing your mind off to the fact that sometimes more risk means that the money you have could be lost.

Sometimes, unrealistic expectations can cause you to go into retirement too soon or spend too much when you're in retirement. So, I try to provide a realistic, clear understanding of what you can expect, based on my 25+ years of experience in the business. It's all a part of the process.

> **InvestWaves here.** What we got from this last chapter shared by our industry veteran, is you need the right MOTIVE to be successful in investing. Greed is a terrible thing, and is sure to kill your performance. Let's see what else he has to share....

CHAPTER 7

THE BIGGEST MYTH EXPOSED

THE PHONE RINGS. It's about 10:00AM and I'm in the middle of a project, at a point where I'd rather not be disturbed. My assistant is out so I need to answer.... Oh well, maybe a break will do me good. 'How can I help you?'

'Hi, this is Harry Wholesaler from Wesure Beatum Investment Company!! Do you have a minute?' Boy, this one is enthusiastic.....

'Sure, but just a minute. I'm in the middle of something right now.'

'No problem, I appreciate your time! We are a money management firm that you can send your clients' money to. We'll do the actual management part, and you can do what you do best – schmooze people and get them to give you even more money for

US to manage! I'm calling to see who you send your clients' money to for management services now, and if you are looking to make any changes.'

'Well Harry, I appreciate your call, but I don't really use third-party advisors. I've found they don't do a very good job, in my opinion, of protecting clients' money. I do the work myself. Plus, if you knew me very well, I'm not really that good of a schmoozer....'

'Really....' Was that sarcasm in his voice? *'Well, tell me about your strategy...'*

I explain the basics of InvestWaves. *'Tell me Harry, does your firm go to cash when the markets are falling?'*

'Well of course not. It's not possible to time the markets. Don't you realize what happens if you miss just the **TEN BEST DAYS OF THE MARKET**.

Me, trying to hide my exasperation. *'I do Harry, but tell me, what happens if I miss the ten WORST days of the market?'*

'That would be impossible. No one is that good.'

'Well Harry, you are telling me that it IS possible to miss all ten of the good days, a random set of numbers in a series, but not possible to miss another, completely random, set of numbers in the same series of days? Statistically speaking, the odds are the same

either way. One is just as likely as the other....and quite frankly, I get a little tired of hearing the 'ten best days' schtick. I wish someone would do the math on missing the ten worst days for a comparison.'

Harry, now sounding a little less chipper. *'You're not interested in using our service, are you?'*

'No Harry.'

'Well, since I know that, I'll tell you that I actually HAVE run the numbers on missing the ten worst days – the returns are astronomical. But of course, it's not possible either way. On that point you are correct. Statistically you have the same odds either way.'

Speaking with Harry was therapeutic for me. It was the first time a wholesaler (an investment company representative who calls on advisors to get them to use their investments or services with clients) dropped their veneer and was completely open with me. He went on to share that the reason third-party advisors DON'T do what I do – preserve client assets by going to cash – is that there are rules that prohibit them from charging a fee if the client isn't fully invested. **<u>Yeah, they don't go to cash because they can't charge you for it. They will instead let your account decline.</u>**

Over the years since I first spoke with Harry, I

have encountered many publications and articles that reinforced that conversation, and I'd like to share some of what I learned from them.

The first article I'm going to talk about is one that annoys me—a lot. It's one I've shared before, with both clients and listeners on my radio show, as I think it highlights some glaring flaws in the mindset of typical investors. The article is called "Develop a Long-Term Plan and Stay Invested."

Why would advisors want to develop a plan that would make you stay invested? Because they make more money if you do and it is less work for them, bottom line.

I actually had a local investment advisor tell me that he didn't have to do what I do in order to make a good living—so why should he have to work that hard?

How about for your clients' wellbeing, for starters?

"Well," he starts to go into it, "what you try to do is impossible. If you miss the 10 best days, etc. etc." as he begins to rehash the familiar adage.

I'm beginning to hear this with some frequency again. Every time the market starts to go down, your typical advisor will bring out these old statistics, such as can be found in the aforementioned article. It starts off with the subtitle "The cost of market timing." And they show that from 1995-2014, the cost of timing the market – essentially looking at the S&P 500 from 1995 to 2014 and staying fully invested in those 5,040 trading days—means that there is an average annual return of 9.9%. If you had missed the 10 best days of the market, your return would have fallen to 6.1%. And that's a significant amount– essentially you would have made 33% less money.

If you're really bad at investing, and you miss the 20 best days, it falls to a 3.6% annual return. And if you miss the 30 best days out of the 5,040? Your return is 1.5%. Your odds get increasingly worse. If you miss the 50 best days, or a mere 1% of the 5,040 investing days, your returns fall to -2.2%. Advisors will use this information to tell you to just buy the stock or mutual fund and hold on to it. Just ride it out!

The next article is a little more honest. Written back in 2007, the author argues that "It's impossible to miss the 10 best days in just 10 years." Unlike the previous article, this one discusses a shortened length of 10 years as opposed to the nearly 20 years from the previous article. The author then figured out the odds of missing all of the 10 best days in the market.

The odds of this occurring are 1 in 2.8 billion billion BILLION. Yes, you read that right—the chances that you will miss the 10 best days of the market over a 10-year span are 1 in 2.8 quadrillion. He said that those odds are comparable to winning the Powerball jackpot with a single ticket purchase BACK TO BACK TO BACK. Winning the Powerball 3 times in a row by buying just ONE ticket each time. It's just not going to happen.

By the same calculation, it's equally impossible to completely avoid the 10 worst days. Again, he compiled illustrative numbers to show how this would work out. In this instance, his time frame is a little bit different – July of 1997 to June of 2006. This period of time wasn't a great time, economically speaking. This was the period that included the boom and bust of the tech bubble crash. To demonstrate, he shows what it would have been like to invest one dollar in the S&P 500. This is not something that you can do, of course—you can't invest directly in the index, and he's not accounting for charges and fees; the author is simply making a point. One dollar invested in the S&P 500 from July of 1996 to June of 1997 would be worth $2.24. Missing the 10 best days, it would be worth $1.40, a 37% drop in your return. However, missing the ten worst days makes your dollar worth $3.67. That is a 64% improvement. So by missing the 10 best, you get 37% less return; missing the 10 worst, you get a 64% gain in your return. The potential benefit of missing the 10 worst days is better than the potential loss of missing the 10 best days, which have a greater impact on returns. Now, the author did say either one is statistically impossible. And while this approach is not something, we strive to do at my office, our strategy does attempt to put the odds in our favor.

The next article I want to discuss is by an advisor-analyst. It dates back to March of 2014, so it's a little more recent than the other two articles. In discussing those who peddle the "Buy and Hold" approach, the author writes that "first, supporters of the buy and hold approach suggest that market returns are random and unpredictable."

When you hear that, you can usually come to this obvious conclusion: that is, you simply cannot predict the 10 best days of the market. Logically, then, this also means that you can't predict the 10 *worst* days either. Pointing out such a next-step logical deduction is usually when I get the dumb-eyed stares of industry people who try to use the "missing the 10 best days" argument with me. When

I point it out to regular folks that I deal with every day, more often than not a lightbulb goes on. It makes sense.

To continue, the advisor-analyst recaps the theory of most "Buy and Hold" investors. First, their theory is that market returns are random and unpredictable. Second, he points out their emphasis on the fact that if you miss the 10 best days in the markets, your returns would be substantially lower than if you were continuously invested. Therefore, since the 10 best days are such rare occurrences, but the impact of missing them is so substantial to your returns, the only prudent approach to ensure you're in the market for these best days is to stay continuously invested.

He then asks the glaringly-obvious question: Why is this so misleading? In what he calls the "Missing the 10 Best Days Myth," the author writes, "Despite the belief by many in the buy and hold camp, that market returns and volatility are random and unpredictable events, the evidence shows what is referred to as volatility clustering. More specifically, we find the vast majority of extreme up and down days occur in bear markets." Pause and think about that for a minute. What the analyst says, and actually proves, is that the biggest up days, historically, tend to occur when the market is tanking. He says that this happens in bear markets because investors' emotions get amplified. This is true. Think back to any periods of hysteria in critical politico-economic times: "This is the bottom! BUY BUY BUY!"

I've heard this already, during the recent market correction; when the market rolls over and starts going down, people are afraid. Fear – FEAR –is the driver in bear markets. FOMO, or fear of missing out. It's not just a phrase thrown about by millennials or, as my daughter informs me, a "New York City Cliché"—if this is the bottom, you want be buying; buy low and sell high, you don't want to miss out! When it's falling, you don't want to be holding, so it's SELL SELL SELL! Fear is the emotion driving these moves.

The advisor-analyst did another study of the S&P 500 index, again looking at the nominal values of hypothetical returns from the index as a good way to gauge the opportunities that are available. From January 1 of 2000 to Dec 31 of 2013, 19 of the 20 best/worst day combinations occurred during the bear markets of 2001-2003, the '08 correction, and the 2011 correction. NINETEEN of those 20 occurred during a bear market correction. Now,

InvestWaves is designed to keep us out of those types of markets. So, if we're doing our job right, my clients are going to miss the majority of those worst days.

Of course, we're probably going to miss the majority of the 10 best days too. But when you consider that both sets – best and worst—occur when markets are *falling*, I don't think I want to be involved in either one of them. And remember— while the odds are 1 in 2.8 billion billion BILLION that you could even miss the best and worst days, they're only random on the individual days; **_they tend to cluster and occur during bear markets._**

This is counterintuitive to most people. You mean the BEST days occur when the markets are falling? One would think that the best days occur when the markets are rising. But when you look at a chart, when the markets are healthy movement is smooth, and day to day increments are nominal, generally trending up. When you hit that volatility, that's often a sign that the markets are getting ready to change direction. So he writes, "the misleading part of the 'Missing the 10 Best Days' argument is that in order to get the majority of the best days, you not only have to experience the majority of the worst days in close proximity, but you also have to be continuously invested throughout the bear markets." So, if you want to catch the best days, you have to stay in the bear markets to do it.

Best and worst days tend to cluster together in terms of timeframe, but they also overwhelmingly occur in bear markets. But what is more important to focus on is the best and worst periods. This is the heart of InvestWaves. We don't try to pick the best days. And people will argue, "Well, you can't time the markets, so how can you predict the best and worst periods?" If by "timing the markets" you mean picking the exact top and the exact bottom – no, you cannot. I tell new clients all the time – the markets will roll over and begin to go down before we will think about getting out. The markets will bottom out and start going back up before we think about getting back in, because we recognize that the market moves in periods that are commonly referred to as bull and bear market cycles. The author goes on to say that these cycles are not completely random and unpredictable, as one cycle inevitably follows the next. Timing the exact tops and bottoms isn't the goal but understanding how to navigate them is more important to your long term returns than worrying about missing the best days. The focus is not on trying to time the market, but rather on trying to align ourselves with the market by using a rules-based, objective, unbiased, and unemotional approach to investing. We call it InvestWaves.

Finally, some people will argue "Well, if your theory is so good, then why isn't everybody doing it?" Well, one of the reasons is, they don't make as much money. The industry, as a whole, does not make as much money because advisors earn higher fees for equity accounts than they do for money market accounts. And the other reason, gratefully, for why they don't do it is because if everybody adhered to this principle, it would cease to work. If everyone runs over to one side of a ship, what happens? The ship tips over. If everyone tried to exit the market at the same time, we wouldn't have a market. That's not an orderly market, and for that reason the exchanges often have triggers – if the market declines to a certain point, they just stop trading. So I am thrilled that not everyone is doing this – because it would make my job impossible. Once it becomes mainstream, it won't work anymore.

The last article I want to talk about was put out by a mainstream mutual fund company that advertises on the radio all the time, and they call their article "The Tale of 10 Days." They state that "for years conventional investment wisdom discouraged market timing strategies by warning investors that missing the market's 10 best days would drag down the value of their portfolios. But the best days are only part of the story, as it turns out. Over the past 84 years, the market's worst days had a far greater effect on portfolio returns. Clearly, investors need to hear both sides of the story."

When I read this article, I was in disbelief—not only did it make sense, but it was also from a mainstream mutual fund company. The company did a study from 1928 to 2011, saying that a $1 dollar investment in 1928 would have grown to $71.20 in 2011, under a "Buy and Hold" strategy that captured performance of each and every day including the 10 best and 10 worst. Obviously, missing positive performance will lower returns. If you miss the 10 best days of market performance in those 84 years, $1 dollar would have grown to only $23.62. About 1/3 of the growth for the entire period – and this is the basis for the warning "Don't miss the 10 best days."

But what happens when an investor misses the 10 worst days? In that scenario, a $1 dollar investment would have grown to $226.14 – more than tripling the overall growth of a "Buy and Hold" strategy. This illustrates that losses can have a disproportionate impact on portfolio return. What is the guiding principle of InvestWaves? Possibly the best way to improve investment returns over time is to avoid large losses. And here it is, in this mainstream publication.

What if an investor avoided the extremes altogether? Again, this goes back to the idea we just discussed of clustering. The numbers show that the best and worst days happen very close to each other. Down 2% today, up 2.5% tomorrow, down 3% the next day—volatile swings that are driven by emotion. With InvestWaves we try to avoid them. What happens if an investor avoided extremes altogether? Missing both the 10 best and 10 worst days would have resulted in a return of $75.01 on a $1 dollar investment. That's $3.84 *more* than the returns of a "Buy and Hold" strategy, with less volatility. Now let me ask you – what good is earning 15 -20% over time, if the ride is so rough that it destroys you emotionally and you can't hang on? By avoiding the best and worst days of bear markets, you may see MORE money with less volatility.

CHAPTER 8

10 MARKET TRUTHS

THIS CHAPTER IS GOING to discuss 10 universal truths about the market. The markets can be misleading—especially the financial markets. I read a funny quote the other day from someone that said:

"If you don't read the news, you're uninformed; if you read the news, you're *mis*informed."

And that's really true when it comes to the financial markets.

Especially considering a recent discovery I made about financial news shows like CNBC. Did you know that the guys that go on there actually PAY to be on there? You think you're watching unbiased news reporting, but when you have these guests – they pay like 50 grand to be on the show, just so they can get some exposure. It's advertising to them. You think the guys on CNBC are out there reporting the "unbiased, unvarnished" news so that you can make good investment decisions, but that's not what they're doing at all. They're selling air time, which puts a whole different spin on it. I'm not against that – by all means, sell air time! But don't make it seem like it's news; that's misleading.

Another thing that's been misleading over the years is the way advisors approach the markets, and what they tell their clients when the markets are down. When I was trained way back in the '80s, when I got into the business, they sat me down in a classroom and taught me how to invest people's money. I'm not referring to the mechanics of investing. When you get licensed, you don't learn how to invest people's money as far as the RIGHT way to do it, you learn the mechanics of _HOW_ to do it. But when I got hired by the insurance company, they sat me down in a room with a bunch of other guys, where they were supposed to teach us the finesse and skills required to really navigate the markets, and they said, "Okay, here's what you do. You put x% in stocks, and x% in bonds, and x% in international, and the reason you do that is because there's something called the Capital Asset Pricing Model that is the foundation for all investing."

In order to comply with the Capital Asset Pricing Model, what an advisor had to do was ask the client a series of questions to determine their risk tolerance. If any of you have invested with a mutual fund person, or an insurance person, I'm sure you've filled out one of these forms before, because it's required. So after you fill out these forms, advisors will take that information and determine your risk tolerance. Now, as I discussed in my previous chapter, I *also* want to determine my clients' risk tolerance—but for a different reason. Let's say that an advisor evaluates your profile and determines that your risk tolerance is 20%. That means you can handle, psychologically, a 20% fluctuation in the value of your investments on your way to whatever goal you want to reach. Based on that, they determine that a 20% fluctuation will give you x% of return on average over the years, and, if you want to average 15% a year, then you have to learn to accept the 20% fluctuation in prices.

This is the foundation of the Capital Asset Pricing Model. And the idea is that they try to quantify risk. The theory is that higher returns equal higher risk. If you don't want high risk, you have to accept the lower return, and if you want a higher return, you have to accept a higher risk.

It's complete nonsense.

It's complete foolishness.

And it's been debunked.

I actually have reports in my office – a major international money management firm did a study looking at the Capital Asset Pricing Model—and they found that it began to break down in the '90s. It doesn't really work anymore.

The guys who came up with this theory – William Sharp and Harry Markowitz –won the Nobel Prize. It worked for a time, but things changed. I should also mention—they came up with this theory in the 1950s. It was devised in the 1950s but they still call it "Modern Portfolio Theory." If you hear an investment advisor talk about Modern Portfolio Theory, they are talking about an idea that was promulgated over 65 years ago.

Essentially, with Modern Portfolio Theory, all an

advisor has to do is look at the standard up-and-down deviation of a center point of an investment and assign it a risk factor; then, they can plug it into a portfolio and say to their client, "You're going to average x% of return with this much risk." That's all they have to do.

That is so lazy. That is BEYOND lazy.

But everybody does it.

I was at a conference in Florida a few years ago, and we're sitting at a table having dinner, and all these guys are talking about their portfolios. They are all using the Capital Asset Pricing Model, and they're all bragging about how "even though the markets were down 50%, their clients only lost 40%." And I'm sitting there, just listening and thinking – you're bragging that your clients only lost 40%? Your clients lost 40%! When the discussion got around to me and it was my turn to speak, I said "Well, we went to cash on such and such a date..." And the group, baffled, simply went "Oh..." and the discussion blew past me. They didn't ask me how I knew to go to cash, or the why behind it. Nobody wanted to know.

I've had local advisors with similar reactions. This is not to disparage my local colleagues, with whom I have formed great relationships. We always say hello when we see each other on the streets and inquire about each other's families. But I was having a cup of coffee with a local guy a while ago, and he said, "How do you do what you do?"

So I showed him.

"Wow," he said, "That looks like it take a lot of time."

"Yes, it does..." I replied.

Pause...

"So anyways, how're the kids?"

Again, he flew by me. What I do takes a lot of work and it's hard, whereas these guys just plug numbers into a model. But hey, they did win the Nobel Prize...

Let's go back into some more recent history. Remember Long Term Capital Management? They were a hedge fund that almost brought the economy to its knees 15 or 20 years ago because they used a risk model to try to invest. They tried to quantify the risk, theorizing that they could manage the risk by having investments in X asset class and investments in Y asset class. They were Nobel Prize winning economists when they came up with this theory that they were using, and it blew up in their faces. They were so leveraged, meaning they had borrowed so much, they believed so much in their model (well, they believed in it, plus the model didn't make any money for them unless they were leveraged) that the end was catastrophic. It blew up so badly, they owed so many people so much money that it was like a domino effect that threatened to cripple the world markets; the US government had to step in and bail them out. I guess the takeaway from all of this is that you don't want to be investing with any Nobel Prize winners, because they screw up!

I had my breakthrough moment in the 90s, it was right around 1994-95. I'm investing the way the insurance company investment guy told me to do it, trained me to do it, but I see that stocks are going down, bonds are going down, internationals are going down…where's the diversification? Where's this asset allocation saving my clients from losing money? The truth was, it *wasn't*. I was frustrated, I was confused, and I would ask my supervisors – what do we do?

"Well," they would tell me, "you just get your clients to hold on. Just tell them to hold on and they'll be fine. The markets always come back."

I didn't get investment advice on how to manage a client's money from my supervisors; instead, I got psychological advice on how to not lose a client, how to counsel people through losing money, how to profit off of a client by manipulating them into keeping their investments in a bad market. Their motto was essentially "Losing money is okay and that's just a part of the investment process."

And it is, to be clear. Let's just put this out there —if you can't stomach some loses, you shouldn't be investing in the markets at all. But this wild notion that the markets can just fall to the floor and that you should just ride it out – that's foreign to me. I don't get it.

A few weeks ago as of the time of this writing, we went to cash – and the markets have been falling ever since. Now, can they go up? Absolutely – and they're going to go up before I get back in. That's just the way we do it. We never get people out at the top, we always wait for it to roll over, and we *measure* market performance. We don't try to guess, we don't use theories, and I don't have any Nobel Prize winners on staff. And when the markets bottom out and begin to strengthen, we measure the strength, and if it looks like it's a good move up, then we get back in.

Sometimes, it looks like it's good and it strengthens and then falls away from us. We're not always right. I mean, *I'm* always right, but sometimes the markets are wrong (I'm kidding, of course!). But in the end, the markets are running the game and they are by nature very unpredictable. I always try to steer clear of guys who try to predict the markets, because as I've discussed in previous chapters, you CAN'T predict the markets.

What you *can* do is MEASURE the markets. And when the markets don't look good, what are you doing in them?

It's like when I used to live in California, and we'd go to the ocean, there were just some times that the waves were too big to be out in the surf. I used to like to body surf. And when you're a certain age, you're invincible! The biggest waves will oftentimes give you the best ride!

One time I caught one of those nice waves, and it flipped me over, and I could feel my feet bouncing off the top of my head, and it hurt. I knew I was in trouble. Fortunately I didn't get seriously hurt, but it taught me a lesson – if it doesn't look safe, it probably isn't safe. And I've carried that over into the way I look at the markets and investing. The market is always going to have its ups and its downs, we're not always going to be right, but there are times when it just doesn't look right. And you always err on the side of caution.

So with that in mind, I want to present you with the 10 market truths:

1. **The market tends to return to the mean—the average—over time.** To do that, it has to go higher than the average at times, and it has to go lower than the average at times– that's why there's an average. Let's say, for example, that the markets average to 12% a year, and you've had a year where the markets were up 20% - that means that the markets are at some point in the future going to have to go well below the average of 12% in order to meet the average. That means you're going to have to have a large loss somewhere along the way.

2. **Excesses in one direction will lead to an opposite excess in the other direction.** So if the markets rise higher than normal, they are going to fall lower than normal.

3. **There are no new eras.** Excesses are never permanent. I remember in the 2000s they talked about a new era of investment in computers and the internet and how that was going to

change everything. It changed nothing. Now they're talking about a new era of employment numbers, and they're managing the economy in a new way—its bologna. There's no such thing as a new era.

4. **Exponential, rapidly rising or falling markets usually go further than you think but they do not correct by going sideways.** So if you've had a huge run up, you better expect a huge drop. It's not just going to stay there and go sideways. It will correct, it will go down. And the higher the rise, the harder the fall.

5. **The public always buys the most at the top and the least at the bottom.** This is probably the biggest one. Everyone wants to buy low and sell high, and nobody does it. Even pro money managers have trouble with this one.

6. **Fear and greed are stronger than long-term resolve.** Let's say you buy

a sock, and it goes down, and you get afraid, so you sell it. Then it turns around and explodes, because every reason you bought it was valid, but you got afraid when it was going down and sold it at the wrong time, because why? Go back to number 5. So you got out at the wrong time, you got stung, and the next time it starts to happen you say "you know what, I'm staying in!" But it goes even lower than the last time, so you panic and get out again, and you lose even more of your money.

7. **Markets are strongest when they are broad and weakest when they are narrow to a handful of blue chips.** Don't base any decision on the DOW – I don't care what the DOW does, it's 30 stocks. You're better off looking at the S&P 500. The list that I watch—the Broad Market—includes over 2,500 stocks, which will give you a much more well-rounded pool of data to base your decisions off of.

8. **Bear Markets have 3 Stages:**

sharp down, reflexive rebound, and a drawn-out fundamental downturn. I believe we're currently on Stage 2 – reflexive rebound from the March 2009 lows. We're not fully down yet. I think we're still in the rebound. We may have started the drawn-out stage, I don't know that yet. Then again, I don't predict, I measure.

9. **When all the experts agree, and all the forecasts agree, you can almost always guarantee that something else is going to happen.** Watch the talking heads on CNN and CNBC, and when they all agree that something is going to happen, you can bet that something *else* is going to happen.

10. **Bull Markets are a lot more fun than bear markets—but you can make money in both.**

InvestWaves here again. Well, as we said from the beginning this isn't a 'perfect' book. Hopefully you were able to get a firmer grasp on the reality of our investment world and have gained a little more confidence in your own intuition about how things really work. Remember – protecting your money has to be the first priority. Avoiding large losses can be THE key you've been looking for to unlock truly life changing gains in your portfolio.

In closing, don't be afraid to leave the herd. They're going to get eaten. And don't let self-serving advisors tell you you're fully clothed in investing myth and jargon. If you feel a draft, well.....

Good investing!

CHAPTER 9

COULD INVESTWAVES WORK FOR YOU?

WHICH LINE WOULD you want representing YOUR portfolio?[1]

If you want to dive in a little deeper, then head over to our website and read some of our blog posts.

1. *Trading involves substantial risk of loss and is not suitable for everyone. You must be aware of the risks and be willing to accept them in order to invest. This is neither a solicitation nor an offer to Buy/Sell securities. No representation is being made that any account will or is likely to achieve profits or losses. The past performance of any trading system or methodology is not necessarily indicative of future results. The SPY is an Exchange Traded Fund whose goal is to closely match the performance of the S&P 500 Index. Invest-Waves utilizes specific Buy/Sell signals and securities purchases based on proprietary models. Flat lines indicate when an account would be 100% in cash. The time period depicted is 8/31/2006 to 8/26/2011. The graph depicted is based on simulated or hypothetical performance results that have certain inherent limitations. Unlike the results shown in an actual performance record, these results do not represent actual trading. Also, because these trades have not actually been executed, these results may have under-or over-compensated for the impact, if any, of certain market factors, such as lack of liquidity, fees and/or commissions. Simulated or hypothetical trading programs in general are also subject to the fact that they are designed with the benefit of hindsight. No representation is being made that any account will or is likely to perform as shown. It should not be assumed that the methods, techniques, or indicators presented will be profitable or will not result in losses. Past results of any trading strategy are not indicative of future returns by that strategy, and are not indicative of future returns which could be realized by you. In addition, the above chart is provided for informational and educational purposes only and should not be construed as investment advice. Such set-ups are not solicitations of any order to buy or sell. Accordingly, you should not rely solely on this Information in making any investment. Rather, you*

should use the Information only as a starting point for doing additional independent research in order to allow you to form your own opinion regarding investments. You should always check with your licensed financial advisor and tax advisor to determine the suitability of any investment. InvestWaves, LLC

www.ingramcontent.com/pod-product-compliance
Lightning Source LLC
Chambersburg PA
CBHW070808220526
45466CB00002B/591